By Julia Donaldson

Illustrated by Axel Scheffler

Run, Stick Man!

Can you colour in the scene?

First published in the UK in 2012 by Alison Green Books
An imprint of Scholastic Children's Books
Euston House, 24 Eversholt Street, London NW1 1DB
A division of Scholastic Ltd
www.scholastic.co.uk
London – New York – Toronto – Sydney – Auckland
Mexico City – New Delhi – Hong Kong
Based on *Stick Man*, the original picture book
by Julia Donaldson and Axel Scheffler

Special thanks to Amy Turner, Vicki Hamilton
and Kim Pedder for their salt dough creations.

ISBN: 978 1 407132 68 6

Printed in China.

1 3 5 7 9 10 8 6 4 2

Papers used by Scholastic Children's Books are made from
wood grown in sustainable forests.

This book belongs to:

Splish, Splash!

Who's this paddling on the river? Join the dots to find out.

You will need:
50g butter
100g dark chocolate, broken into small pieces
2.5tbsp golden syrup
80g cornflakes

Large saucepan
Spoon
Cupcake cases

Easter Nests

Lots of birds live in the family tree. Here's a recipe to make your very own tasty bird nests.

What to do:

1. Place the butter and the chocolate pieces in a large saucepan with the golden syrup.
2. Slowly melt over a low heat and keep stirring.
3. When the mixture is completely melted, turn off the heat.
4. Add the cornflakes to the saucepan and stir well.
5. When the cornflakes are well covered in chocolate, place some small paper cupcake cases on a tray.
6. Fill each case with a heaped tablespoon of the mixture.
7. You can decorate your nests with chocolate eggs, or any other kind of sweet you like.
8. Put in the fridge to set.

Always ask a grown-up to help you when you're cooking.

Spot the Difference

There are five differences between these two scenes. Can you spot them all?

Answers: In the left hand picture there is a cat instead of a pigeon; the sun is missing; the girl on the bench has a pink top; the dog is missing; the child throwing Stick Man is missing.

Who lives in the Family Tree?

There are 4 pieces missing from this jigsaw. They're all in the sticker section at the back of the book. Find them and complete the jigsaw of the Family Tree!

Little Bird Lost

The baby swan can't find her nest. Can you help her?

Twitch, twitch!

Join the dots to find out who has such long ears.

I'm not a Pooh-Stick!

Can you colour the scene?

You will need:
2 cups of plain flour
1 cup of table salt
1 cup of water

Spoon
Bowl
Baking tray (optional)

Salt Dough

Salt dough is a kind of modelling clay, great for making sculptures and decorations.

MAKING

1. Put the plain flour and salt in a mixing bowl.
2. Add the water, bit by bit, and keep mixing with a spoon until you make a soft dough.
3. If the dough feels too sticky, add more flour. If the dough feels too dry, add more water.
4. When the dough is mixed together, remove from the bowl and place on a flat surface.
5. Ask a grown-up to help you knead the dough for 5 minutes to help create a smooth texture.
6. If you can, let the dough stand for approximately twenty minutes, before beginning a project.

Then, get modelling!

Always ask a grown-up to help you when you're cooking.

DRYING

1. You can either dry your salt dough naturally in the open air, or you can bake it in the oven.
2. To dry it in the oven, put your models on a baking tray in the oven at 50°C/120°F for 30 minutes, then increase the temperature to 100°C/210°F/Gas 1/4. It'll take 3 or 4 hours to dry in the oven. When your model is dry, turn off the oven and leave it inside to cool down.
3. If you decide to leave your dough to dry naturally, it will take between 30 and 48 hours. Turn your model over once it has dried on one side, so the other side can dry, too.

Then, get decorating!

Stick Man's Top Tips

- Don't put your salt dough in your mouth – it'll taste horrible!
- You can use acrylic paints or poster paints to decorate your dough, or even felt-tip pens.
- Unused dough can be stored in the fridge, in an airtight container or cling film, for up to a week.

Cheese Sticks

Stick Man's favourite snack is . . .

Cheese Sticks! You can make some, too.

You will need:

50g self-raising flour
25g softened butter
80g finely grated Cheddar
or Red Leicester cheese
20g freshly grated Parmesan

Large bowl
Rolling pin
Non-stick baking tray
Wire rack

What to do:

1. Preheat the oven to 200°C/400°F/Gas 6. Grease the baking tray, or line it with baking parchment.
2. In a large bowl, mix the flour, butter and both kinds of cheese together by hand. It might look crumbly but that's okay. Keep kneading it all together until you make a ball of dough.
3. Sprinkle some flour on a board or work surface. Place the dough on the floured surface and, using the rolling pin, roll it to 1/2 cm thick.
4. Cut your cheesy dough into strips, about 2cm wide and 12cm tall. You can use cookie cutters to make other shapes, too.
5. Place the sticks on the baking tray, then put them in the oven for 8-10 minutes.
6. When they're done, transfer your sticks to a wire rack to cool.

Stick Man's Top Tips

You can also make this dough in a food processor. Just whizz all the ingredients together till they form a ball of dough.

Always ask a grown-up to help you when you're cooking.

Make your own Stick Man bunting

You will need: scissors, glue, 1.5m string, ribbon or cotton

1. Cut around all the coloured triangles.
2. Fold along all the dotted lines.
3. Take one triangle. Carefully glue along the tab at the top, then fold it over the string or ribbon, starting 15cm from the end.
4. Repeat with all the triangles until you have a lovely string of bunting to hang in your room! (See picture overleaf.)

Ask a grown-up to help when you're using scissors.

glue along these tabs

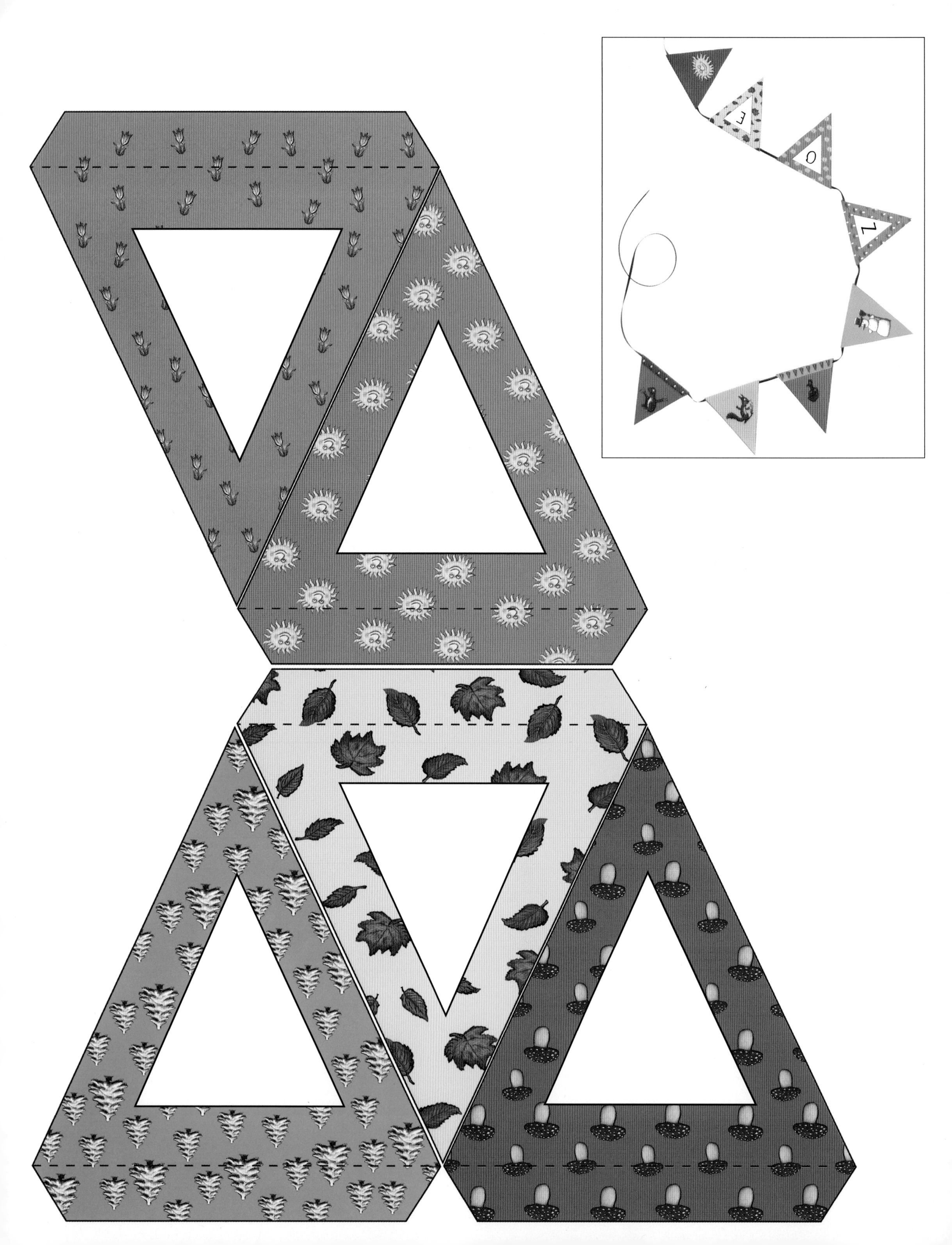

Draw a picture in the white spaces, or write your name, putting one letter in each triangle.

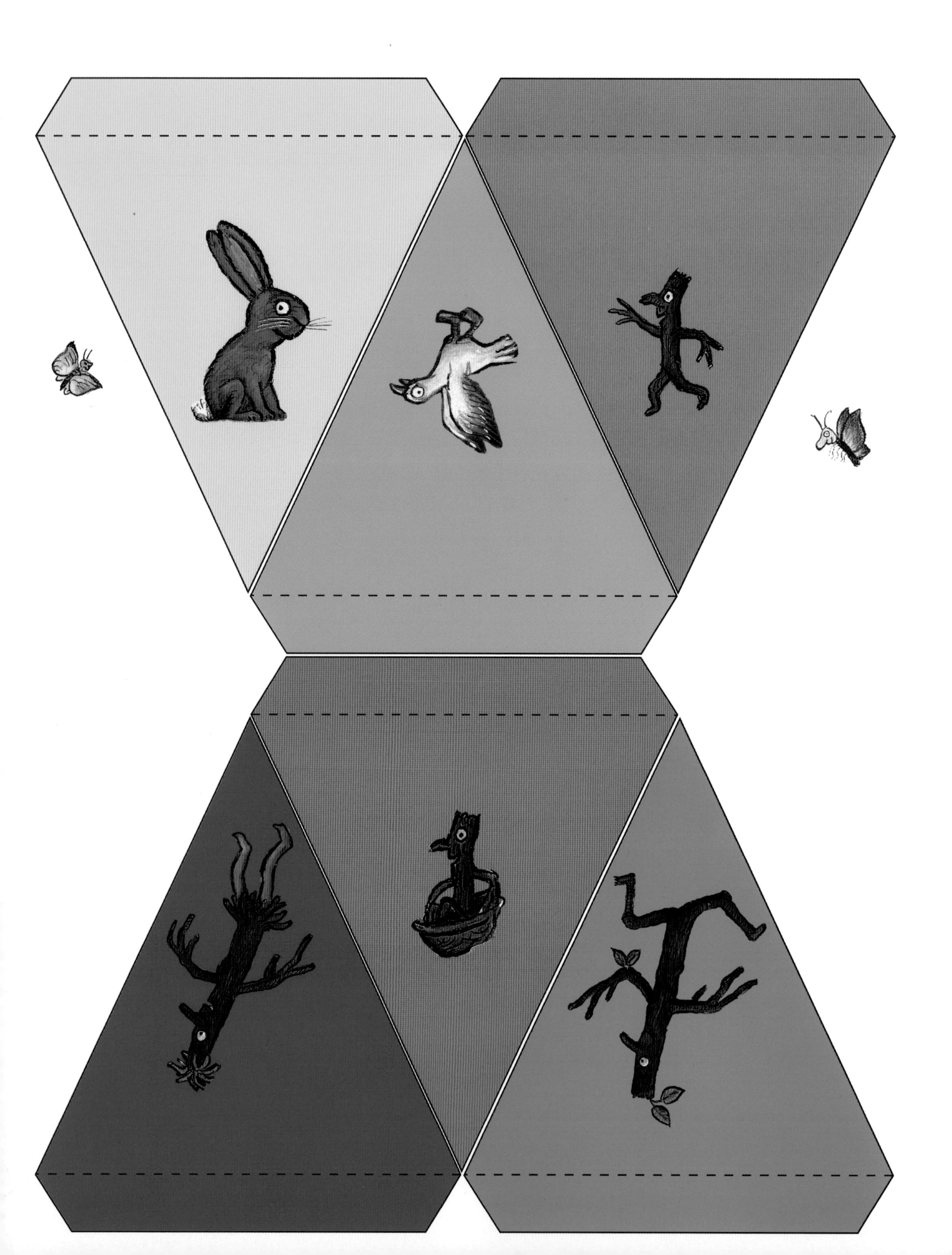

Summer Word Search

There are five summery words for you to find. We've found one to get you started - can you find the other four?

Row, Row, Row Your Boat

Can you colour in this river scene?

Going Jogging

Who could this be running through the park?

Join the dots to solve the mystery.

Draw a Beach Scene

Can you add to this summery scene? You could draw a sun in the sky, a sandcastle, or even people playing.

Pink Lemonade

Always ask a grown-up to help you when you're cooking.

Stick Man gets very thirsty jogging through the park. His favourite drink is nice, ice-cold pink lemonade. Here's the recipe:

You will need:
- 100g caster sugar
- 150g raspberries
- 1 lemon
- 1 orange
- Lemonade or water
- Saucepan
- Bowl
- Sieve

What to do:

1. Ask an adult to cut the lemon and the orange into slices.
2. Place the raspberries, sugar, orange and lemon in a large saucepan.
3. Pour over 300ml cold water.
4. Bring to the boil, stirring every now and again. Turn the heat off and leave to cool.
5. Place a sieve over a bowl or pan, and pour the mixture through.
6. Push down on the fruit with a spoon to get all the juices out.
7. The syrup you collect will be the base for your pink lemonade.
8. To serve, pour a little of the pink syrup into a glass and top up with lemonade or still water.

Stick Man's Top Tip:

If you put your pink lemonade syrup in the fridge, it'll keep for about a week.

Tu-Whit
Tu-Whoo!
Who's this sitting on the branch? Find out by joining the dots!

Fun at the Beach

Can you colour in this sunny scene?

Spot the Difference

There are five differences between these two scenes. Can you spot them all?

Answers: In the top picture, the top left-hand house is blue; the girl is wearing a yellow jumper; one duckling is missing; the bird on the rock is missing; and there is a stick missing on the river.

Stick Man is Lost!

Which line will lead him back to the Family Tree?

Answer: B

Zzzzz!

Stick Man is lying on the fire! Who's this sleeping next to him?

The Stick Family

Here's a picture for you to colour in.

Match the Shadow

Can you match the shadows to the right pictures?

Bedtime in the Family Tree

There are 4 pieces missing from this jigsaw. They're all in the sticker section at the back of the book. Can you find them and complete the scene?

You will need:

For the cakes:
100g softened unsalted butter
100g self-raising flour
100g caster sugar
2 medium eggs

For icing and decoration:
100g icing sugar
70g very soft butter
40g cocoa powder
30ml milk
1 teaspoon vanilla extract
Liquorice laces
Sweets to make eyes

Mixing bowl
Whisk (hand or electric)
Cupcake cases
Wire rack
Cocktail stick

Spider Cupcakes

There are lots of creepy crawlies in the branches above the family tree. Follow this recipe to make your very own tasty spiders!

To make the cakes:

Preheat the oven to 180°C/380°F/Gas 4.

1. In a large bowl, whisk the butter, flour, sugar and eggs until they form a creamy mixture.
2. Spoon 2 tablespoons of the mixture into each cupcake case and place them in a muffin tin. Cook for between 10 and 15 minutes. They'll turn a golden-brown colour when they're ready.
3. Place on a wire rack and leave to cool.

To make the chocolate icing:

4. In a bowl, mix the icing sugar, butter, cocoa powder, milk and vanilla extract until it forms a smooth icing.

To decorate your cakes:

5. Once the cakes are cool, spread your chocolate icing on them.
6. Next, make eight holes around the edge of your cake with a cocktail stick, as shown in Picture 1.
7. Cut your liquorice laces into strips about 5cm long and poke one into each of the holes in the cake, as shown in Picture 2.
8. Stick two small sweets on to the icing to make the eyes. Finally, using your cocktail stick, put a dot of the icing on the sweets to make the pupils.

Picture 1

Picture 2

Always ask a grown-up to help you when you're cooking.

A Stick for the Fire!

Can you colour this scene?

Owl is perched in the tree all on her own. There are lots of birds in the sticker section at the back of the book. Can you find them and put them in the tree, too?

Winter Word Search

There are five words hidden in this word search. One has already been circled for you - can you find the other four?

BELLS

SANTA

S	N	O	W	F	P
A	I	T	L	N	H
N	W	H	B	V	A
T	R	E	E	X	T
A	S	J	E	Q	Y
G	B	E	L	L	S

SNOW

TREE

HAT
(already circled)

Ho-Ho-Ho!

Look who's just come down the chimney!
Can you colour in Santa in his festive red suit?

Jingle Bells
Jin-gle bells! Jin-gle bells!
Jin-gle all the way. Oh, what fun it
is to ride in a one-horse op-en slei-gh!
Jin-gle bells! Jin-gle bells! Jin-gle all the
way. Oh, what fun it is to ride in a
one-horse op-en sleigh!

Can you sing along with Stick Man's favourite Christmas carol? You could try playing it on the recorder, too.

You will need:

125g butter

50g caster sugar

175g plain flour

Icing sugar to decorate

1 tablespoon milk

Large bowl

Rolling pin

Baking tray

Cookie cutters

Wire rack

Shortbread Stars

The Stick family always leave these shortbread stars out for Santa when he visits – they're his favourite!

What to do:

1. Using the tips of your fingers, rub the butter, caster sugar and flour together in a big bowl until it looks like breadcrumbs.
2. Add a tablespoon of milk to the mixture.
3. Ask an adult to knead the mixture for a minute or two until it forms a smooth ball of dough.
4. Put the dough in the fridge for half an hour to rest.
5. Roll out the dough on a floured surface until it's about 1cm thick.
6. Using a cookie cutter, cut out your biscuits and place them on a baking tray.
7. Bake at 180°C/360°F/Gas 4 for 12-15 minutes.
8. When the biscuits are golden brown, remove from the oven and place on a wire rack to cool.
9. Sprinkle with icing sugar.

Always ask a grown-up to help you when you're cooking.

Ask a grown-up to help when you're using scissors.

Paperchains

Decorate your bedroom with these Stick Man paperchains.

See over the page for instructions.

- Carefully cut out your paperchains along the dotted lines.
- Take one paperchain. Use glue or sticky tape to make it into a loop.
- Take another paperchain. Slot it through the first loop, and use glue or sticky tape to stick the ends together.
- Carry on, adding each strip of paper, until you have a complete chain.

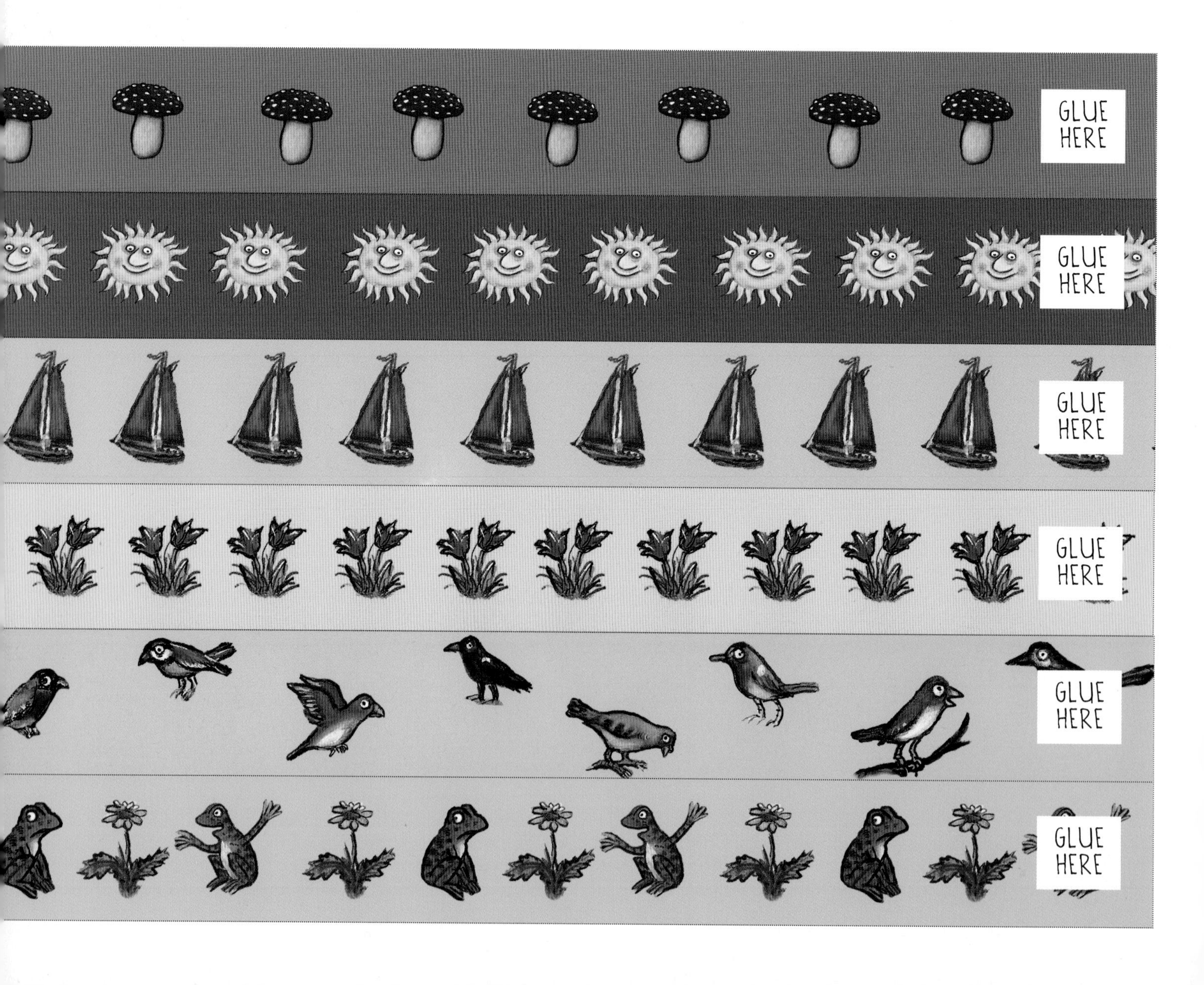

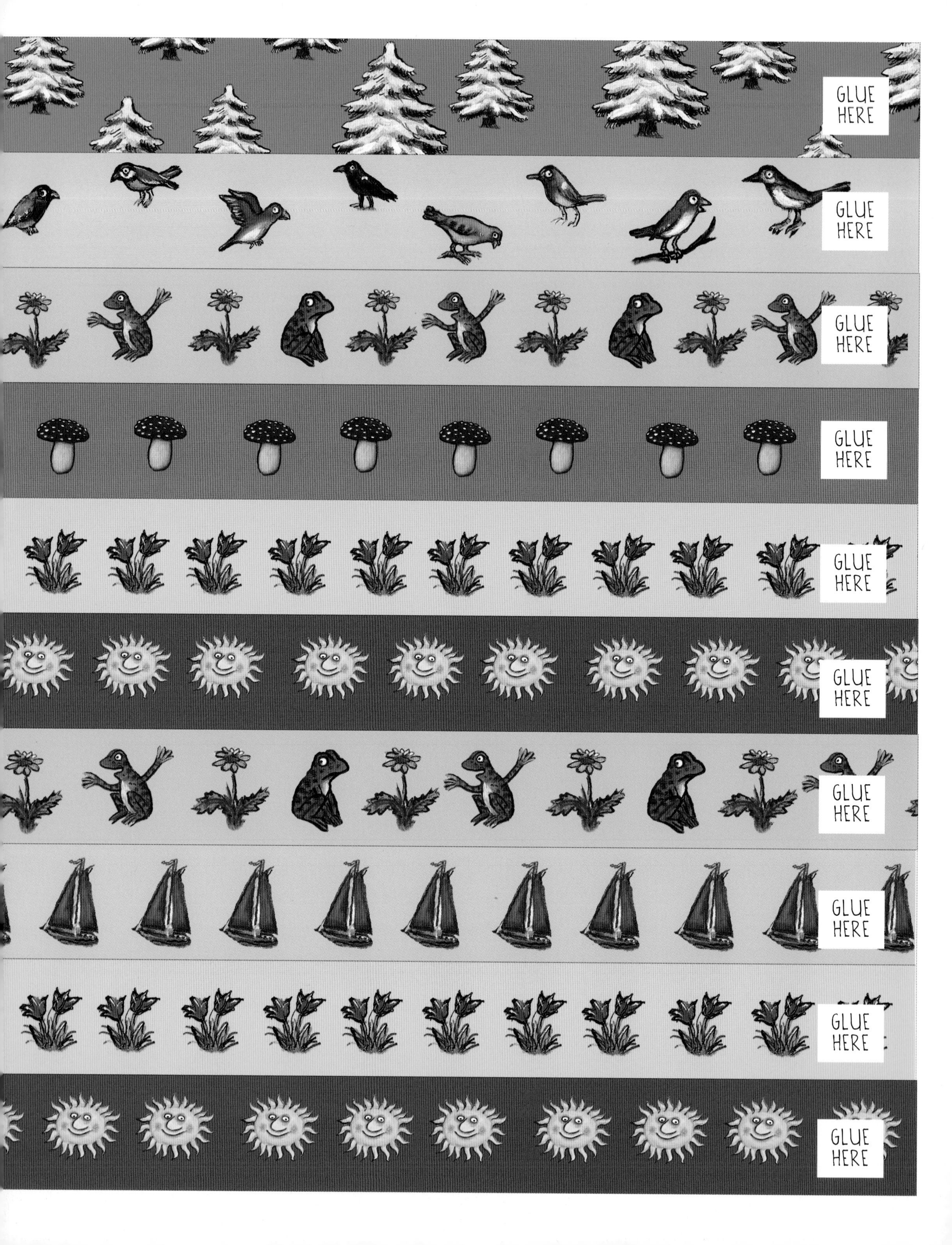
GLUE HERE
GLUE HERE
GLUE HERE
GLUE HERE
GLUE HERE
GLUE HERE
GLUE HERE
GLUE HERE
GLUE HERE
GLUE HERE

Draw a Snowy Scene

Can you add to this snowy scene?

You could draw a Christmas tree, a snowman or even Stick Man.

Brrr!

Who's this with a carrot for his nose? Join the dots to find out.

Jingle! Jingle!

What's that noise up above? Can you colour in this picture of Santa and his merry reindeer?

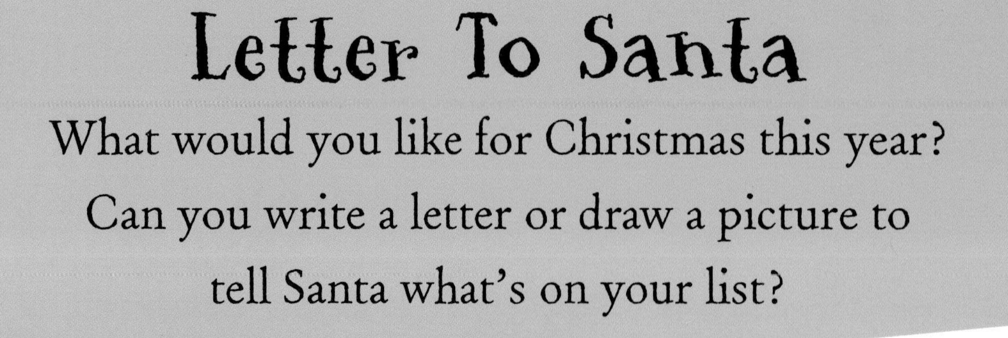

Letter To Santa

What would you like for Christmas this year?
Can you write a letter or draw a picture to
tell Santa what's on your list?